marina
GERMAIN

TRAVEL JOURNAL
Seychelles

Bibliographic information of the German National Library: The German National Library lists this publication in the German National Bibliography; detailed bibliographic data are available on the Internet at http://dnb.dnb.de.

Layout, photos, illustrations, Proofreading:
Marina Germain, www.ellaworks.de

Publisher: BoD · Books on Demand GmbH, In de Tapen 42,
        22848 Norderstedt, bod@bod.de

Printed by: Libri Plureos GmbH, Friedensallee 273, 22763 Hamburg

The German version is available here: **www.ellaworks.de**

ISBN: 978-3-7693-5237-5

IMPRINT

This

TRAVEL JOURNAL *Seychelles*

belongs to

WHO COMES WITH ME...

....

OUR TRIP STARTS ON ....

FROM THIS AIRPORT ....

THE RETURN TRIP IS ON ....

This is my ...

○ **1.** trip to Seychelles

○ **2.** trip to Seychelles

○ **3.** trip to Seychelles

○ .... trip to Seychelles

I have already been to these **islands**

○ Mahé ➜ not only airport

○ Praslin

○ La Digue

 ....

 ....

 ....

On this **trip** I would like
to see these *islands*

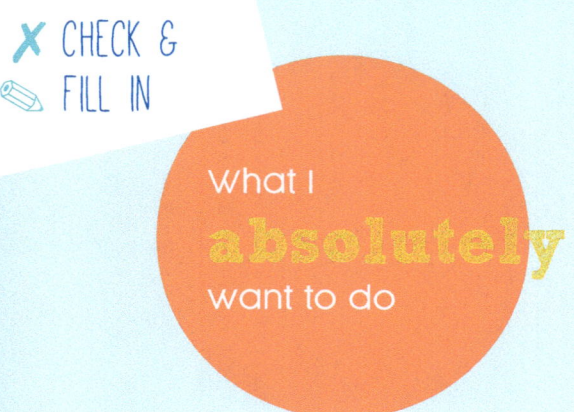

What I
absolutely
want to do

○ Stroking the giant tortoise

○ Eat from the breadfruit

○ Dancing on the beach

○ Walk around the island

○ Take part in a beach clean-up

○ Taste Seybrew & Takamaka Rum

○ Enjoy the moment

○ Spot a turtle
(but don't disturb them!)

○ Close my eyes and hold my face in the sun

- Hug a palm tree
- Watching birds
- Feel the perfect happiness
- A boat trip
- A bus trip
- Come back again

This has to go in the **suitcase**

SEYCHELLES

today

 DATE ....

 ISLAND ....

 ACCOMMODATION ....

WHAT HAPPENED TODAY

....

....

....

....

....

....

....

....

....

....

....

....

....

....

....

THE WEATHER TODAY

HIGHLIGHTS OF THE DAY

HOW WAS THE FOOD?

today

 DATE ....

 ISLAND ....

 ACCOMMODATION ....

WHAT HAPPENED TODAY

THE WEATHER TODAY

HIGHLIGHTS OF THE DAY

HOW WAS THE FOOD?

today

 DATE ....

 ISLAND ....

 ACCOMMODATION ....

WHAT HAPPENED TODAY

THE
WEATHER
TODAY

HIGHLIGHTS OF THE DAY

HOW WAS THE FOOD?

Recipe for HAPPINESS

LOVE

FREEDOM

NATURE

SUNSHINE

FOOD

TIME

HEALTH

PEACE

MUSIC

NICE PEOPLE

All I need is

Vitamin Sea

today

 DATE ....

 ISLAND ....

 ACCOMMODATION ....

WHAT HAPPENED TODAY

THE WEATHER TODAY

HIGHLIGHTS OF THE DAY

HOW WAS THE FOOD?

today

 DATE ....

 ISLAND ....

 ACCOMMODATION ....

WHAT HAPPENED TODAY

....

....

....

....

....

....

....

....

....

....

....

....

....

....

....

THE WEATHER TODAY

HIGHLIGHTS OF THE DAY

HOW WAS THE FOOD?

today

 DATE ....

 ISLAND ....

 ACCOMMODATION ....

WHAT HAPPENED TODAY

THE WEATHER TODAY

HIGHLIGHTS OF THE DAY

HOW WAS THE FOOD?

Typical
islanders

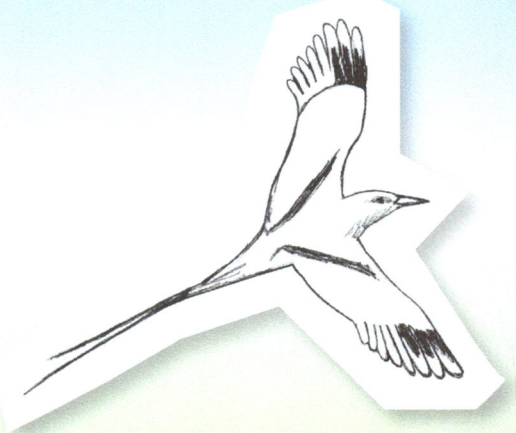

○ MADAGASCAR FODY

○ WHITE-TAILED TROPICBIRD

○ TORTOISE

○ MANTA RAY

DISCOVERED

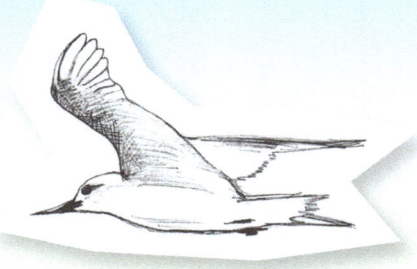

○ FRUIT BAT

○ WHITE TERN/
FAIRY TERN

○ TENREC

○ GECKO

○ TURTLE

today

 DATE ....

 ISLAND ....

 ACCOMMODATION ....

WHAT HAPPENED TODAY

THE WEATHER TODAY

HIGHLIGHTS OF THE DAY

HOW WAS THE FOOD?

today

 DATE ....

 ISLAND ....

 ACCOMMODATION ....

WHAT HAPPENED TODAY

THE WEATHER TODAY

HIGHLIGHTS OF THE DAY

HOW WAS THE FOOD?

today

 DATE ....

 ISLAND ....

 ACCOMMODATION ....

WHAT HAPPENED TODAY

THE WEATHER TODAY

HIGHLIGHTS OF THE DAY

HOW WAS THE FOOD?

MAKE SOME

photos
memories
doodle

HAPPINESS

SEA

today

 DATE ....

 ISLAND ....

 ACCOMMODATION ....

WHAT HAPPENED TODAY

....
....
....
....
....
....
....
....
....
....
....
....
....
....
....
....
....
....
....

THE
WEATHER
TODAY

HIGHLIGHTS OF THE DAY

HOW WAS THE FOOD?

today

 DATE ....

 ISLAND ....

 ACCOMMODATION ....

WHAT HAPPENED TODAY

....

....

....

....

....

....

....

....

....

....

....

....

....

....

....

....

....

....

THE WEATHER TODAY

HIGHLIGHTS OF THE DAY

HOW WAS THE FOOD?

My favorite pics

today

 DATE ....

 ISLAND ....

 ACCOMMODATION ....

WHAT HAPPENED TODAY

....

....

....

....

....

....

....

....

....

....

....

....

....

....

....

....

....

THE WEATHER TODAY

HIGHLIGHTS OF THE DAY

HOW WAS THE FOOD?

today

 DATE ....

 ISLAND ....

 ACCOMMODATION ....

WHAT HAPPENED TODAY

THE WEATHER TODAY

46

HIGHLIGHTS OF THE DAY

HOW WAS THE FOOD?

today

 DATE ....

 ISLAND ....

 ACCOMMODATION ....

WHAT HAPPENED TODAY

THE
WEATHER
TODAY

HIGHLIGHTS OF THE DAY

HOW WAS THE FOOD?

Happiness

is walking on the beach

our **holiday hitparade**

We played this **music** up and down

1 Singer / Band:
Song:

2 Singer / Band:
Song:

3 Singer / Band:
Song:

4 Singer / Band:
Song:

5 Singer / Band:
Song:

6 Singer / Band:
Song:

today

 DATE ....

 ISLAND ....

 ACCOMMODATION ....

WHAT HAPPENED TODAY

....

....

....

....

....

....

....

....

....

....

....

....

....

....

THE WEATHER TODAY

HIGHLIGHTS OF THE DAY

HOW WAS THE FOOD?

today

 DATE ....

 ISLAND ....

 ACCOMMODATION ....

WHAT HAPPENED TODAY

THE WEATHER TODAY

HIGHLIGHTS OF THE DAY

HOW WAS THE FOOD?

Thoughts
Moments

Memories

Mahé

Carana Beach

Glacis

Sunset
Beach

Beau
Vallon

Anse Major

Victoria

Sainte
Anne

Moyenne

Long

Cerf

Port
Launay

The International
Airport

Conception

Port
Glaud

Thérèse

Grand
Anse

Anse aux
Pins

Anse
Boileau

Pointe
au Sel

Anse la
Mouche

Anse
Royale

Baie
Lazare

Anse
Forbans

Anse
Intendance

Police
Bay

My highlights on Mahé

My highlights on Praslin

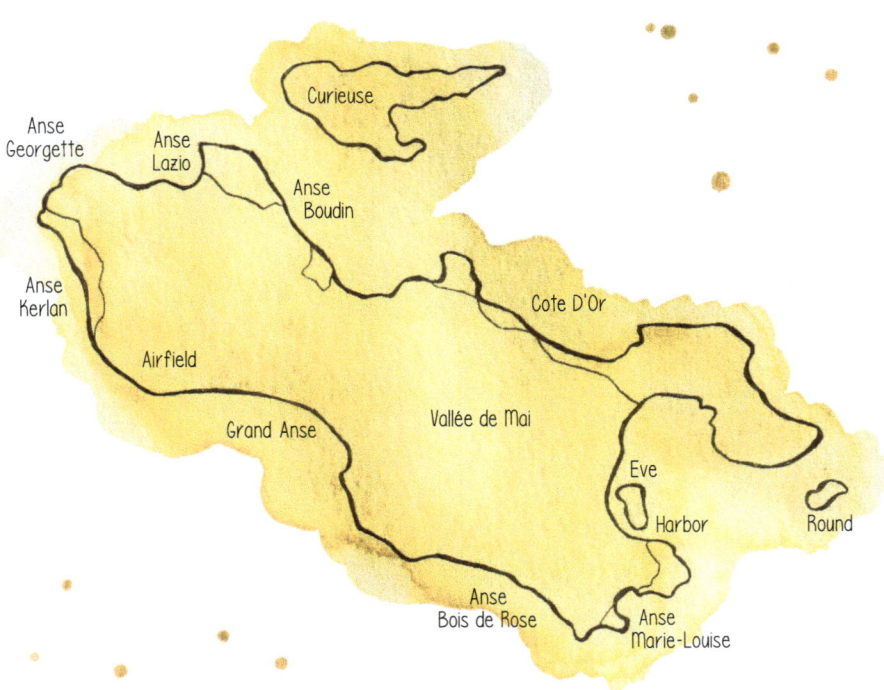

Curieuse

Anse
Georgette

Anse
Lazio

Anse
Boudin

Cote D'Or

Anse
Kerlan

Airfield

Vallée de Mai

Grand Anse

Eve

Harbor

Round

Anse
Bois de Rose

Anse
Marie-Louise

la Digue

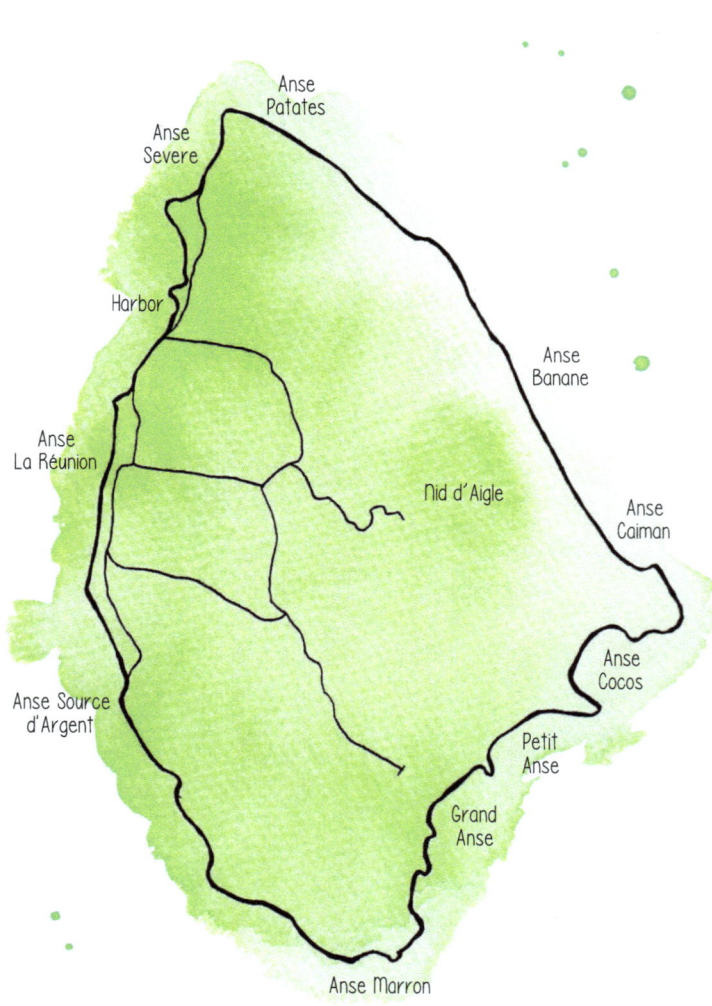

Anse
Patates

Anse
Severe

Harbor

Anse
La Réunion

Nid d'Aigle

Anse
Banane

Anse
Caiman

Anse
Cocos

Anse Source
d'Argent

Petit
Anse

Grand
Anse

Anse Marron

My highlights on La Digue

Sea

the beauty in life

My *Favorite places* in Seychelles

This is my
favourite island:

....

I still want to see these
islands: